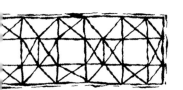  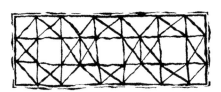

WORLD
RELIGIONS

FACTS ABOUT
ISLAM

Alison Cooper

New York

Published in 2011 by The Rosen Publishing Group Inc.
29 East 21st Street, New York, NY 10010

Copyright © 2011 Wayland/
The Rosen Publishing Group, Inc.

First Edition

Original designer and illustrator: Celia Hart
Layout for this edition: Jane Hawkins
Consultant: Dr. Fatma Amer

Library of Congress Cataloging-in-Publication Data

Cooper, Alison.
 Facts about islam / Alison Cooper. — 1st ed.
    p. cm. — ((World religions))
 Includes index.
 ISBN 978-1-61532-322-7 (library binding)
 ISBN 978-1-61532-327-2 (paperback)
 ISBN 978-1-61532-334-0 (6-pack)
 1. Islam—Juvenile literature. I. Title.
 BP161.3.C67 2011
 297—dc22

                                    2009052445

Photographs:
Front cover, Corbis; Axiom Photographic Agency,
p. 19(b) (James Morris); Circa Photo Library
(ICOREC), p. 25(b); Ronald Grant Archive, p.
13(t); Sonia Halliday Photographs, pp 34, 38;
Michael Holford Photographs, endpapers;
The Hutchison Library, pp. 23(b), 42, 43
(Macintyre); The Image Bank, p. 27(t)
(Carlos Navajas); Impact Photos, p. 8(b)
(Ian Cook); Bipinchandra J Mistry, pp.
16(r), 21(t); Only Horses Picture Agency,
p. 35(t); Christine Osborne Pictures, pp.
15(t), 16(1), 22, 24, 25(t), 27(b), 33(t).
33(b) 35(b), Ovidio Salazar, pp28, 29(t);
Peter Sanders Photography, pp. 8(t), 9,
12, 13(b), 14, 15(b), 17, 20, 21(b), 23(t),
29(b), 31, 32, 36, 37, 41; Trip, pp. 30, 40.

Endpapers: This eighteenth-century
Persian carpet has a pattern of
flowers and leaves.

Manufactured in China
CPSIA Compliance Information: Batch #WAS0102YA: For Further
Information contact Rosen Publishing, New York, New York at 1-800-237-9932

CONTENTS

WHO ARE THE MUSLIMS?

A Muslim is someone who follows the religion of Islam. Muslims believe in the oneness of God (Allah in Arabic). They honor

Muhammad (PBUH) as the final Prophet (PBUH) of Allah and messenger of Islam. There are several groups of Muslims and they each have slightly different beliefs. The two biggest groups are Sunni Muslims and Shia Muslims.

◀ The Shahada

The Shahada is the declaration of faith that every Muslim learns. It says, "I bear witness that there is no God but Allah, and I testify that Muhammad (PBUH) is His Messenger." Part of the Shahada is written on the flag of Saudi Arabia, which is shown in the photograph on the left.

Traditional Dress ▶

Many Muslims prefer to wear traditional dress, like those in the photograph. There is no specific type of Islamic dress, but women may only show their hands and face and men must also dress modestly. Muslims living in Western countries often choose to wear Western-style clothes.

Germany
Russia
UK
France
Albania
Kazakhstan
Morocco
Turkey
China
Iran
Algeria
Libya
Egypt
Saudi
Arabia
India
Thailand
Sudan
Pakistan
Malaysia
Philippines
United
States
Guyana
Surinam
Ghana
Nigeria
Democratic
Republic
of the Congo
Somalia
Kenya
Tanzania
Zambia
Madagascar
Mozambique
South Africa
Indonesia
Bangladesh
Australia

Proportion of
population that
is Muslim

Over 75%

50–75%

10–50%

1–10%

Argentina

There are 25 countries in which more than
95% of the population is Muslim.

The Islamic World ▲

There are 1.5 billion
Muslims. Most Muslims live
in the Middle East, Africa,
and Asia. In North Africa and
the Middle East, almost the
whole population is Muslim.
There are also large numbers
of Muslims in Russia, India,
and some European countries,
especially Bosnia, Bulgaria,
and Albania.

✳ MUSLIM EMIGRATION TO EUROPE ✳

Many Muslims have emigrated to Europe to
look for work or to study, especially since the
1950s. Often, they have emigrated to countries
that had a link with their own country in the
past. There are many Pakistanis in the UK,
for example, because Great Britain once ruled
the area that is now Pakistan.

▲ Islamic Education

At this Islamic school in London, UK,
Muslim children also learn Arabic so that
they can read their holy book, the Koran
(Qur'an). They learn how to pray and they
have breaks from classes at prayer times.
Their school uniform allows them to cover
their bodies according to Islamic rules.

TIMELINE

571 C.E.	610 C.E.	622 C.E. 1 A.H.	632 C.E. 11 A.H.	634–644 C.E. 13–23 A.H.	644–656 C. 23–35 A.H.
The Prophet Muhammad (PBUH) is born to the Quraysh tribe, who were guardians of the holy Kaaba.	The angel Gabriel tells the Prophet (PBUH) that God wants him to spread His word.	The Prophet (PBUH) leads his followers to Medina. The Muslim calendar begins.	The Prophet (PBUH) dies. Abu Bakr Siddiq is elected first Khalifa.	Reign of Khalifa Umar. The Middle East and Iran are conquered.	Reign of Khali Uthman. The Koran is compiled on h orders.

◀ The Kaaba shrine in Mecca

Tile decorated with the name of Khalifa Uthman ▶

1588–1629 C.E. 996–1038 A.H.	1526 C.E. 932 A.H.	1453 C.E. 857 A.H.	1389 C.E. 791 A.H.	1258 C.E. 656 A.H.	1169–1193 C.E. 564–589 A.
Islam spreads to Southeast Asia.	Babur starts the Mongol Empire in India, which lasts for more than 300 years.	The Ottomans capture Constantinople and rename it Istanbul.	The Muslim Ottomans win control of the Balkans.	Baghdad is destroyed by Mongol invaders.	King Richard of England begins the Third Crusade against the Muslims of Palestine.
C.E. 1683 1094 A.H. The Ottomans attack Vienna.					

◀ The Blue Mosque, Istanbul

1757 C.E. 1170 A.H.	1798 C.E. 1213 A.H.	1802–1805 C.E. 1217–1220 A.H.	1881–1885 C.E. 1306–1329 A.H.	1924 C.E. 1342 A.H.	1928 C.E. 1348 A.H.
Muslim power in India grows weaker as the British become stronger there.	The French general, Napoleon, captures Egypt.	Muslims rebel in Arabia because they think Islam is not being followed strictly enough.	Mahdi sets up a Muslim state in Sudan.	The Ottoman Caliphate is abolished.	Hasan al Banna, a Sufi sets up the Muslim Brotherhood to create an Islamic state.

The Kingdom of Saudi Arabia

The holy city of Mecca (Makkah in Arabic) is in the Kingdom of Saudi Arabia. The country's name comes from the desert people who used to rule parts of the region.

The first Saudi ruler, Muhammad Ibn Saud, died in 1765. For almost 200 years, his descendants defended Mecca from rebels and other countries that wanted to win control of the holy city. In 1926, after winning several battles, Ibn Saud was declared King. The country's name was changed from Hijaz to Saudi Arabia in 1932.

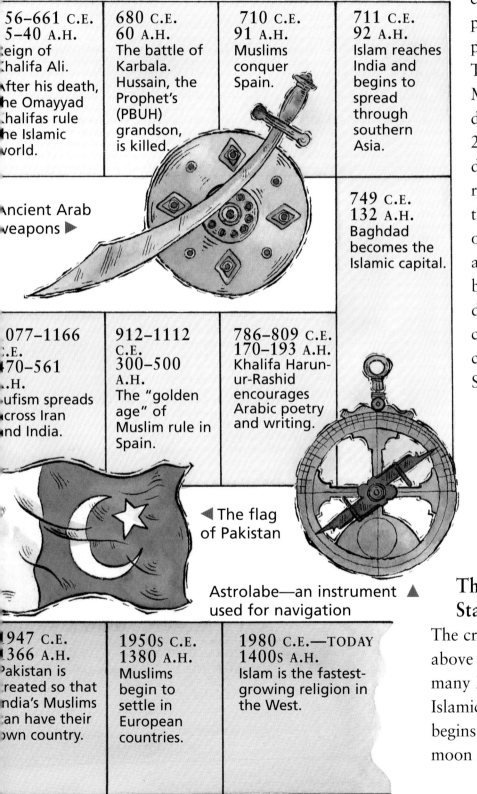

56–661 C.E. 5–40 A.H. eign of halifa Ali. fter his death, he Omayyad halifas rule he Islamic vorld.	680 C.E. 60 A.H. The battle of Karbala. Hussain, the Prophet's (PBUH) grandson, is killed.	710 C.E. 91 A.H. Muslims conquer Spain.	711 C.E. 92 A.H. Islam reaches India and begins to spread through southern Asia.
ncient Arab veapons ▶			749 C.E. 132 A.H. Baghdad becomes the Islamic capital.
077–1166 .E. 70–561 .H. ufism spreads cross Iran nd India.	912–1112 C.E. 300–500 A.H. The "golden age" of Muslim rule in Spain.	786–809 C.E. 170–193 A.H. Khalifa Harun-ur-Rashid encourages Arabic poetry and writing.	
947 C.E. 366 A.H. akistan is reated so that ndia's Muslims an have their wn country.	1950s C.E. 1380 A.H. Muslims begin to settle in European countries.	1980 C.E.—TODAY 1400s A.H. Islam is the fastest-growing religion in the West.	

◀ The flag of Pakistan

Astrolabe—an instrument used for navigation ▲

The Crescent and ▲ Star Symbol

The crescent moon with a star above it appears on the flag of many Muslim countries. In the Islamic calendar, each new month begins when the crescent (new) moon appears.

HOW DID ISLAM BEGIN?

Islam began in 610 C.E., when the Prophet Muhammad (PBUH) received a message from God. Muhammad (PBUH) was born in Mecca in 571 C.E.

When he grew up, Muhammad (PBUH) became troubled by the way the people of Mecca behaved. They treated their slaves badly and often killed baby girls at birth. They worshiped many different gods. Islam came with a message of justice, peace, and love for everyone.

The Message

Muslims believe that when Muhammad (PBUH) was 40 years old, the angel Gabriel came to him with a message from God. He said Muhammad (PBUH) must tell the people of Mecca to stop worshiping false idols and worship the one true God, Allah. Later, he told Muhammad (PBUH) about other Prophets (PBUH), including Abraham (Ibrahim) (PBUH), Moses (PBUH), and Jesus (PBUH).

The photograph on the right shows Mount Hira. It was here, in the cave on the right of the picture, that Muhammad (PBUH) received God's message. Today, many Muslims visit this place of historic importance.

THE CHARACTER OF THE PROPHET (PBUH)

People who knew the Prophet Muhammad (PBUH) said that he was kind and thoughtful. His nicknames were *Al-Sadiq* and *Al-Amin*, which mean "the truthful one" and "the trustworthy." He especially loved children and animals, and respected women and elderly people. He preached love and mercy.

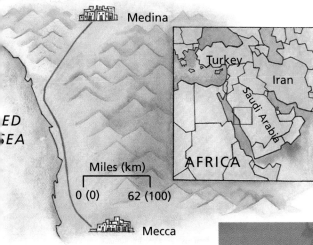

Medina

Turkey

Iran

Saudi Arabia

AFRICA

ED SEA

Miles (km)

0 (0)   62 (100)

Mecca

The Journey to Medina

The people of Mecca hated Muhammad (PBUH) because he spoke out against their gods and their corrupt way of life. After ten years of persecution, Muhammad (PBUH) and his followers had to flee the city. The map shows their journey to Medina.

Battles ▶

The photograph on the right shows a scene from the 1976 movie, *The Message*, which tells the story of the beginning of Islam. There were battles between the people of Quraysh and the Muslims in the early years. The first important battle was at Badr in 624 C.E., when 313 Muslims beat 1,000 Meccan soldiers.

The Mosque at Medina

Muhammad (PBUH) became a respected leader in Medina. There he built a simple house and a mosque made of mud brick and thatched with palm leaves. Many people went to visit him and worship in the mosque. After the Prophet's (PBUH) death, the mosque was gradually made bigger. Today, it is a beautiful mosque known as the Mosque of the Prophet (PBUH). The photograph on the left shows a visitor reading the Koran there.

WHAT DO MUSLIMS BELIEVE?

Muslims believe that there are five very important actions that they should perform. These are known as the *Arkan-ul-Islam,* or Five Pillars

of Islam. The first is Shahada, the declaration of faith (see page 8). The second is Salat, the duty to pray five times a day. The third is Zakat, or giving to charity, and the fourth is Siyam, fasting during the month of Ramadan. The fifth is Hajj, which means making a pilgrimage to Mecca.

▲ The Kaaba

The photograph shows the Great Mosque in Mecca. In the center is the black shrine called the Kaaba. Wherever they are in the world, Muslims turn in the direction of the Kaaba when they say Salat (their daily prayers).

BASIC BELIEFS

The basic beliefs of Islam are set out in the prayer *Al-Iman-ul-mufassil* ("the faith in detail"): "I believe in Allah, His angels, His books, His Prophets (PBUH), the Day of Judgement, His power of God Almighty over good and evil, and in life after death."

...slims believe that giving
...harity is a way of
...shiping Allah. Zakat is a
...ation to charity that all
...slims have to pay. A
...ional committee uses the
...ney that is collected to help
...ple in need. Muslims are
...ouraged to help people in
...er ways, too. This girl is
...ing food at a bazaar to
...e money for charity.

...ding the Fast ▶

...e Prophet (PBUH) often ended the Ramadan
... with a pinch of salt, a few dates,
... some milk and honey. These foods
... still served at the end of the fast today.

milk

honey

salt

dates

◀ The Ramadan Fast

Ramadan is the month when
the angel Gabriel gave the first
revelation of the Koran to the
Prophet (PBUH). Muslims mark
this month by going without
food or beverages (fasting)
between sunrise and sunset.
Being hungry and thirsty helps
them to learn to control their
feelings and behavior. The
family in the photograph on
the left are ending their daily
fast with a meal after sunset.

WHAT IS THE MUSLIM HOLY BOOK?

The Muslim holy book is called the Koran (Qur'an in Arabic). Muslims belie[v]e that it contains the exact words of God. These were revealed to Muhammad

(PBUH) when he was in Mecca and Medina. The Prophet (PBUH) would recite the words of God t[o] his followers. They wrote them down right away o[n] parchment, stones, the bark of trees—any material they could find. The Koran tells the stories of Abraham (Ibrahim) (PBUH) Moses (PBUH), and others who also appear in the Torah, the Jewish holy book.

▲ Koran, Prayer Beads, and Prayer Mat
Muslims often read from the Koran after Salat. This is why they sometimes leave the holy book on their prayer mat (*musallah*) with their prayer beads (*sebha*).

A Qari Reciting from the Koran ▶
A Qari is someone who reads the Koran aloud in the mosque, or at any gathering of worshipers. The Qari is greatly respected for his reading skills. The Koran is written in Arabic. Although many Muslims cannot speak Arabic, they have to pronounce the words correctly when they read or pray.

"The Opening" ▶

This is a page from the Koran. It contains the first chapter, called *Al-Fatiha*, or "The Opening." It praises Allah and asks for his help.

The page is decorated with real gold dust and powdered lapis lazuli, a blue stone. The very first Koran was much plainer. Zaid ibn Thabit, the Prophet's (PBUH) secretary, spent many years gathering together its verses from the people who first wrote them down.

ISLAMIC LAW FROM THE KORAN

Koranic law divides human actions into groups:
Fard—things that must be done.
Mandub—actions that are strongly encouraged.
Mubah—actions that are neither punished nor rewarded because the Koran does not mention them.
Makruh—actions that are discouraged.
Haram—actions that are forbidden.

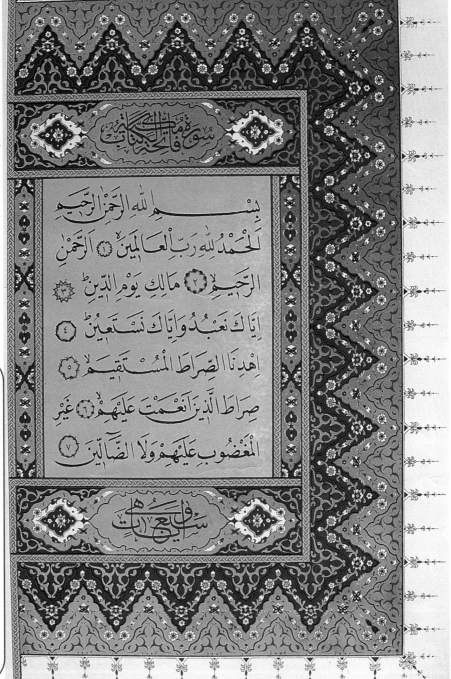

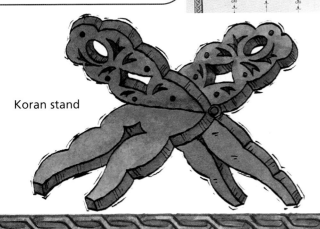

Koran stand

◀ A Koran Stand

Muslims often rest the Koran on a wooden stand like the one shown here. This makes it easier for them to read from the holy book. Some stands are plain, but others are highly decorated.

WHAT IS SUNNA?

The word Sunna means "tradition." Muslims use it to mean the example that the Prophet (PBUH) set for them to follow. "This is my straight path," he said, "so follow it. Do not follow other paths that will separate you from this path. So Allah has ordered you so that you may be truly obedient."

The Sunna is based on what the Prophet (PBUH) said, did, and approved of. It covers many aspects of life, including family life and how to conduct business.

EVERY GOOD DEED IS A CHARITY AND IT IS A GOOD DEED TO MAKE SOMEONE SMILE.

WEALTH COMES FROM A CONTENTED HEART NOT A LOT OF POSSESSIONS.

SAY ALLAH'S NAME (WHEN DINING), EAT WITH YOUR RIGHT HAND, AND EAT FROM THE NEAREST SIDE OF THE DISH.

ALL MUSLIM MEN AND WOMEN MUST SEEK KNOWLEDGE.

VISIT THE SICK, FEED THE HUNGRY, AND FREE THE CAPTIVES.

DO NOT SIT BETWEEN TWO MEN WITHOUT THE PERMISSION OF BOTH.

The Hadith ▲

The Hadith are the sayings of the Prophet (PBUH). You can read some examples above. The Hadith were collected together after the Prophet's (PBUH) death, so that Muslims would always be able to live in the way the Prophet (PBUH) had advised.

THE COLLECTORS OF THE HADITH

The sayings of the Prophet (PBUH) were passed down from people who had known him to later generations of their families. Collectors of the Hadith had to be sure that the sayings had really come from the Prophet (PBUH) himself. One collector, Imam Bukhari, is said to have kept just 6,000 of the 60,000 sayings that people told him were words of the Prophet (PBUH).

Pilgrims ▶

The picture on the right is from a famous book, written around 900 years ago. It shows pilgrims traveling to Mecca. The Prophet (PBUH) told his followers that they should always provide hospitality for travelers. He would go hungry himself if visitors arrived who needed food and beverages.

Islamic Law ▼

The men below are studying the Sharia, the Islamic law. This comes from the Koran. It is explained in the Hadith and in other collections of books known as *Fiqh*.

Perfume Bottles ▼

The Prophet (PBUH) was very fond of perfumed oil called attar. Muslims often keep attar in beautiful bottles and offer it to their guests. One drop behind the ears or on the wrist gives a nice smell.

Perfume bottles

HOW DO MUSLIM FAMILIES LIVE?

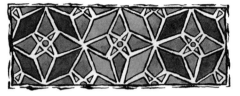

Muslim families live according to the rules set out by their religion. There are rules about how to dress, what to eat, and how to behave. Good manners are very important. According to the Prophet (PBUH), "No father can give his child anything better than manners." Muslims must not gamble, talk about people behind their backs, be lazy, or interfere in other people's business.

◄ Saying Adhan
The man in this photograph is saying the *Adhan* prayer (call to prayer, see page 23) into a newborn baby's ear. The first word the baby hears is "Allah." The baby will be named seven days after it is born.

Rosewater sprinkler

Incense and Rosewater ▶
Keeping clean is important in Islam. Muslims burn sweet-smelling incense after cleaning their homes. On special occasions, they sprinkle guests with rose-scented water.

Incense burner

◀ Bismillah Ceremony

The boy in the picture is learning to read the Koran. In some parts of the world, Muslims hold a ceremony called Bismillah when a child learns to read the Koran for the first time. This often takes place when a child is around four years old. Family and friends gather to hear the reading. It is a very special day.

RULES FOR EATING AND DRINKING

Islamic law divides food into three different types:

Halal—foods that are allowed

Makruh—foods that may be eaten but that Muslims are not encouraged to eat

Haram—foods that are forbidden. These include the meat of pigs and carnivorous animals, certain types of cheese (because animal products are used to make them), and anything that causes addiction, such as alcohol.

Halal Meat ▲

The photograph shows a halal butcher's shop. Halal means "lawful." The butcher has to prepare the meat in a particular way. As he works, he says the words *Allaho-Akbar*, which means "God is great." He removes all the fat and blood from the meat, which keeps it fresh for a longer period of time.

WHERE DO MUSLIMS WORSHIP?

Muslims pray in a mosque whenever they can. The mosque is not only a place of worship. It is also a place where Muslims can meet, share news, and offer support to one another. Worshipers take off their shoes before they enter the prayer hall. Men and women have separate areas for worship.

Regent's Park Mosque ▼

The photograph below shows a mosque in London, UK. It has a courtyard, a dome, and a minaret (a tower). These are common features of mosques all over the world.

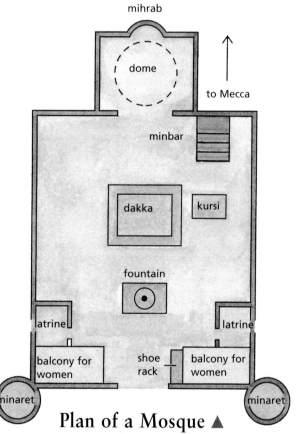

Plan of a Mosque ▲

An arch called the mihrab is set into one wall of the mosque. This shows the direction of the Kaaba in Mecca. The Imam leads the worshipers from steps called the minbar. In large mosques, officials stand on a platform called the *dakka* and copy the prayer actions of the Imam for everyone to follow. Beside the *dakka*, there is a lectern called the *kursi*. The Koran rests on this for recital by the Qari.

◀ Muadhin Calling People to Prayer

This man is a Muadhin. He tells Muslims it is time for prayer by calling the Adhan (see boxed text) from the roof of the mosque. In many mosques, there are microphones in the minarets so that people can hear the call to prayer even if they are a long way from the mosque.

Praying on the Street ▼

Muslims perform Salat five times a day, at dawn, noon, late afternoon, dusk, and after dark. In Muslim countries, they pray wherever they happen to be at prayer time. In the picture below, people have spread out their prayer mats in the city center in Cairo, Egypt.

THE CALL TO PRAYER

Allah is the greatest.
I bear witness that there is no God but Allah.
I bear witness that Muhammad (PBUH) is his Prophet (PBUH). Hasten to prayer, hasten to success. Allah is the greatest. There is no God but Allah.

HOW DO MUSLIMS WORSHIP?

Muslims believe that Allah created people to worship Him. So as well as performing Salat and reading from the Koran,

they often say special words of worship many times throughout the day. They do this to thank Allah, to praise him, and to remember Him before each activity.

Muslims gather together for prayer on happy occasions, such as the birth of a baby. They also pray together on sad occasions—when someone is sick or dies, for example.

◀ **Praying with Prayer Beads**

This woman is doing *tasbih*. She is using sebha, or prayer beads. As she touches each bead, she says one of the 99 names of Allah. Each name has a meaning, such as *Al-Rahman*, "the Merciful," *Al-Aziz*, "the Powerful," and *Al-Hafiz*, "the Protector."

Sebha
(prayer beads)

WORDS OF WORSHIP

Muslims repeat Arabic phrases such as these several times a day:

Bismillah—in the name of Allah

Alhamdo Lillah—praise be to Allah

InshaAllah—if Allah wills

MashaAllah—by Allah's grace.

▲ **Prayer Beads**

Prayer beads are small and easy to carry. There are either 33 beads divided into groups of 11, or 99 beads divided into 33.

Washing Before Prayer ▶

This man is at a country mosque in Thailand. He is performing the washing ritual that Muslims perform before they pray. This ritual is called *wudu*. As well as washing his feet, he must wash his hands, forearms, and face.

Positions for Prayer ▼

These are the four main positions used for prayer when performing Salat. There are ten separate actions altogether, which are repeated. The worshiper repeats the words *Allaho-Akbar* ("God is great") between actions.

standing

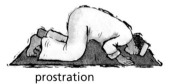

bowing

kneeling

prostration

◀ The Prayer Mat

Many Muslims own a prayer mat like this one. The pictures on it show the Holy Haram at Mecca (top left), the mosque at Medina (top right), and the arch of a mihrab (bottom).

HOW DOES THE MUSLIM CALENDAR WORK?

The Prophet (PBUH) left Mecca and traveled to Medina in the year 622 C.E. This event is called the Hegira migration.

The Hegira marked the starting point of the Muslim calendar and years are counted from this event. During the year, Muslims celebrate important events in their history. These include the Prophet's (PBUH) birth, his last pilgrimage, and his death. All Muslims also celebrate the two festivals of Eid.

❃ ☙ ISLAMIC CALENDAR ❧ ❃

MUHARRAM
The Day of Hegira (New Year)
Commemoration of the battle of Karbala

RAJAB
Isra wal Miraj
(Ascent of Muhammad [PBUH] to heaven)

SAFAR

SHA'BAN

RABI-UL-AWWAL
Maulid-ul-Nabi
(Birthday of the Prophet [PBUH])

RAMADAN
The month of fasting
Lailat-ul-Qadr (God's message
to Muhammad [PBUH])

RABI-UL-AKHIR

SHAWWAL
Eid ul-Fitr
(Feast of Breaking of the Fast)

JAMADA-AL-AWWAL

DHUL-QADA

JAMADA-AL-AKHIR

DHUL-HIJJAH
Hajj pilgrimage at Mecca
Eid ul-Adha (Feast of the Sacrifice)

◄ The Lunar Calendar

Each month in the Islamic calendar begins when the crescent (new) moon appears. When the crescent moon is sighted, the news is broadcast on radio and television. Scientific methods are used to calculate the date when the crescent moon will appear if the weather is too cloudy for the moon to be seen.

The Islamic year is 11 days shorter than the year used in the Western world. This is because the Western year is based on the orbit of the Earth around the Sun instead of on the phases of the moon.

Tazia

The New Year Procession

New Year is a sad time for Muslims. This is when they remember the death of the Prophet's (PBUH) grandson, Hussain. He was killed during a holy war at Karbala on the tenth day of Muharram. The photograph above shows Shia Muslims in Iran, taking part in a procession of mourning for Imam Hussain.

Tazias ▲

In their procession Shia Muslims carry a *tazia*—a model of the tombs of the people who died at Karbala. Some Muslims do not agree with this custom.

WHY IS MECCA IMPORTANT?

Mecca (Makkah) is important because the Prophet (PBUH) was born there. It is also important because the Kaaba is there. According to Islam, Allah told Abraham (PBUH) to build the Kaaba. It was the first shrine built for worship of the One God. All Muslims are expected to make a pilgrimage to Mecca.

The Great Mosque ▼

The Great Mosque in Mecca. The Sacred Enclosure around the Kaaba can hold over 2.5 million pilgrims.

The main pilgrimage, which takes place once a year, is called Hajj (see page 30). Pilgrims also visit throughout the year.

In the late twentieth century, Saudi Arabia became very wealthy from producing oil. Mecca was transformed into a modern city, with many hotels for the millions of pilgrims who visit every year.

THE POSTAL SERVICE

During the two weeks of Hajj the Pilgrims' Postal Service sends out thousands of letters from the pilgrims to their family and friends at home.

Caring for Pilgrims ▶

The officials who are in charge of Mecca try to take care of all the visitors who come to the city, especially for Hajj. There are different grades of hotel so that poor people, as well as rich, can afford to stay. The people in the photograph on the right are camping at the airport between journeys.

Hospitals are provided along the route of the pilgrimage. The crowds are so big that strict health and safety rules have to be followed to prevent disease from spreading, or danger from fire.

Bottles of water

Cakes of mud

Souvenirs ▲

Bottles of water and cakes of mud from the spring of Zamzam near the Kaaba are popular souvenirs. The angel Gabriel opened the spring to provide water for baby Ishmael after Abraham (PBUH) left him there.

Closing for Prayer ▼

The sign below is a common sight in Mecca. As soon as the call to prayer echoes through the city, shopkeepers stop work in order to pray. Muslims often use prayer times as a way of making appointments. For example, they might arrange to meet someone "after the dusk prayer."

CLOSE FOR PRAYER مغلق للصلاة

WHAT IS HAJJ?

Hajj is the pilgrimage that takes place in Mecca between the 8th and the 13th of the month of Dhul-Hijjah. The pilgrims start at the Kaaba and visit various holy sites around Mecca. They then leave the city and follow the route of the Prophet's (PBUH) last journey. They visit Arafat, Muzdali and Mina, where they stay overnight.

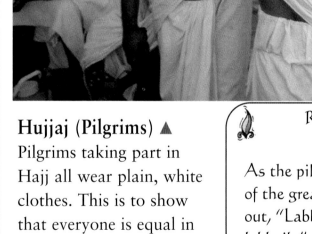

Hujjaj (Pilgrims) ▲
Pilgrims taking part in Hajj all wear plain, white clothes. This is to show that everyone is equal in the eyes of Allah.

READY FOR SERVICE
As the pilgrims enter the gate of the great mosque, they call out, "Labbaik! Allahumma labbaik," which means "Here I am, oh Allah, at your service!" Full of joy, they approach the Kaaba.

Circling Around the Kaaba ▲

Thousands of pilgrims crowd around the Kaaba as Hajj begins. They circle the Kaaba seven times and then pray at the Station of Abraham (PBUH). Abraham (PBUH) is said to have prayed here when he had finished building the Kaaba. Pilgrims visit the Kaaba again at the end of Hajj.

A pattern
embroidered in gold
on the Kiswa ▼

◄ The Kiswa

The Kiswa is the cloth that covers the Kaaba. It is black, with verses from the Koran embroidered on it in real gold and silver. A new Kiswa is put on the Kaaba at Hajj.

Mina ▼

The last stage of Hajj takes place at Mina. The pilgrims in the photograph are throwing stones at three stone pillars, which represent the devil. The festival of Eid ul-Adha is celebrated here, when the pilgrims sacrifice sheep or goats (ideally rams). They do this to remember that Abraham (PBUH) was prepared to obey Allah's instructions and sacrifice his only son, until Allah sent a ram for the sacrifice instead.

WHAT ARE THE MOST IMPORTANT MUSLIM FESTIVALS

The two most important festivals are Eid ul-Fitr and Eid ul-Adha. Eid ul-Fitr is celebrated on the first day of the month of Shawwal. It marks the end of Ramadan, the month of fasting, and the time when the Prophet Muhammad (PBUH) first received the Koran. Eid ul-Adha is celebrated on the tenth day of Dhul-Hijja. This is the Eid of Sacrifice, when a ram is sacrificed as a reminder of Abraham's (PBUH) obedience to Allah (see page 31)

Giving Gifts at Eid ▶

People give gifts to their families and friends at Eid, as the woman in this photograph is doing. They also give gifts of food, money, and clothes to poor people. Giving gifts is a way for Muslims to share whatever God blesses them with.

PRAYER AT EID

Families get up early on Eid morning to bathe and prepare for their visit to the mosque. Special prayers are said in the mosque. After prayers, people visit their friends and relatives to wish them a happy Eid.

◀ Beautifully decorated serving dishes filled with sweet foods ▶

◀ New Clothes at Eid ul-Fitr

The photograph on the left shows children in Cairo, Egypt, wearing their best clothes for Eid. People like to wear new clothes at Eid, especially at Eid ul-Fitr.

Food for Eid ▼

In the photograph below, Lebanese Muslims are having an Eid meal where traditional dishes are being served. Popular dishes include rice, roast meats, and salad. Muslims live all over the world, and they eat their favorite local dishes at Eid.

Sweet Foods ▼

Sweets and cakes, nuts, and dried fruit are offered to visitors at Eid. Muslims like to serve sweet foods on happy occasions, to show that they hope life will be sweet for them.

33

HOW DID ISLAM SPREAD?

At first, Muslim armies spread the Islamic faith to the peoples that they conquered. Later, wise and holy people known as Sufis converted communities peacefully through their teachings. Merchants also spread Islam to traders whom they met on their journeys. By around 1500 C.E., the Muslim world included the entire Middle East and reached into Eastern Europe, North Africa, and India.

◄ The Siege of Vienna

In 1529 C.E., the Muslim armies of the Turkish Ottoman Empire attempted to capture the Austrian city of Vienna. The painting on the left shows them outside the city walls. But just as the city was about to surrender, the Muslims went away—the best of their soldiers wanted to get home to Turkey before winter.

Ottoman Weapons ▼

For more than 300 years, the Ottoman army was the best and largest army in the world. It was also very well equipped. Soldiers wore fine armor and helmets. Their weapons were sometimes beautifully decorated with gold and precious metals, like the ones shown here.

Ottoman daggers

◄ Horse-Riding Festival

The men in this photograph are putting on an exciting display of horse-riding in Morocco. They are taking part in celebrations at the tomb of Moulay Idris, who died in 828 C.E. Islam came to Morocco long before the time of Idris, but he strengthened the faith in the area. Today, all the countries of North Africa are Muslim.

SUFIS

The first Sufis came from Iraq around 800 C.E. The Sufi saints were great teachers who devoted themselves to worshiping God and promoting spirituality. Some of these great leaders helped to spread Islam in the northwestern part of the Indian subcontinent.

Ottoman axes

Mosque in Thailand ▲

Traders brought Islam to Southeast Asia in the Middle Ages. The mosque in the photograph above is built in the local Thai style. It is raised on stilts to prevent it from being flooded.

WHO ARE THE LEADERS OF ISLAM?

The Prophet (PBUH) was the first ever Muslim leader. After his death, religious leaders were called Khalifas (successors). The early Khalifas were wise men, who lived simply in their communities in the way they had always done. Later, as the Muslim empire grew, the Khalifas became very rich and powerful.

Imams ▶

An Imam teaching children about Islam. The word Imam means "someone who guides from the front." Today, it usually refers to a man who leads prayers in the mosque. The Imam must have at least some knowledge of the basic religious teachings. Many Muslim scholars are Imams as well.

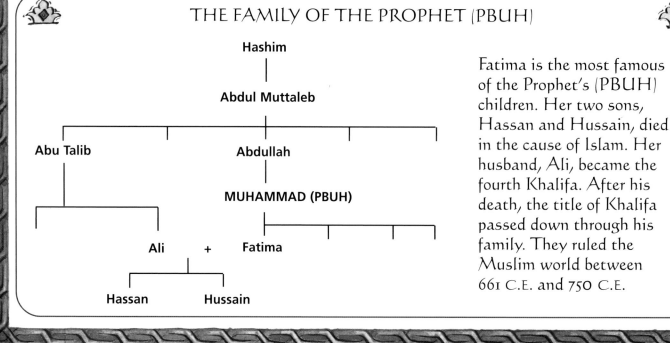

THE FAMILY OF THE PROPHET (PBUH)

Hashim

Abdul Muttaleb

Abu Talib   Abdullah

MUHAMMAD (PBUH)

Ali   +   Fatima

Hassan   Hussain

Fatima is the most famous of the Prophet's (PBUH) children. Her two sons, Hassan and Hussain, died in the cause of Islam. Her husband, Ali, became the fourth Khalifa. After his death, the title of Khalifa passed down through his family. They ruled the Muslim world between 661 C.E. and 750 C.E.

Abu Bakr

Umar

Uthman

Ali

The First Four Khalifas ▲

The pictures above show the names of the first four Khalifas. They were all close friends and advisers of the Prophet (PBUH). The Muslim empire became much bigger while Umar was Khalifa. The Koran was put together in the time of Uthman.

◄ The Hand of Fatima

Shia Muslims sometimes carry models of the "hand of Fatima," like the one shown on the left, in their processions. The four fingers and the thumb represent the Prophet Muhammad (PBUH), Fatima, her husband Ali, and their two sons. Shia Muslims have special respect for Fatima's family.

Shrine of Khawaja Nizamuddin ▶

Khawaja Nizamuddin was a Sufi. The photograph on the right shows his shrine. He set up a religious community, and taught people about Islam and how to praise Allah. Sufis obeyed no one except Allah—not even kings. If a ruler wanted to meet a Sufi, he had to go to the Sufi's humble home.

IS ISLAMIC DESIGN SPECIAL?

Followers of other religions worshiped idols and pictures of their gods, but Islam was against such worship. This was why the first Muslim leaders would not allow their followers to paint pictures of people or animals. Instead, they painted complicated patterns to remind everyone of the amazing world that Allah had created. These beautiful patterns can be seen today on buildings, fabrics, and pottery.

arabesques are based on the natural curves of plants

patterns based on flowers

calligraphy

The Dome of the Rock ▲

The Dome of the Rock in Jerusalem is an important mosque. In the photograph above, you can see the colorful tiles, set in complicated patterns, that cover the walls. Many Islamic buildings are decorated in this rich blue color. The tiles are glazed to make them hard and shiny.

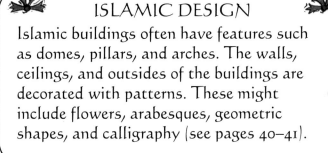

ISLAMIC DESIGN
Islamic buildings often have features such as domes, pillars, and arches. The walls, ceilings, and outsides of the buildings are decorated with patterns. These might include flowers, arabesques, geometric shapes, and calligraphy (see pages 40–41).

◀ Gardens and Fountains

Muslims liked to have cooling fountains in their gardens. These fountains are in the gardens of the Alhambra palace in Spain. The palace was built when Spain was ruled by Muslims, more than 800 years ago.

A decorated plate and vase

Pottery ▶

Pottery objects such as these have been made in the Islamic world for over 1,000 years. Jugs, plates, and vases with this type of design are still made in parts of Spain and North Africa, and they are very popular.

◀ Carpet Designs

The Turkish rug in the photograph on the left is called a vase rug. The whole picture seems to spring from the vase in the center. Other popular designs for carpets are hunting scenes, gardens with birds perching on flowers, and the tree of life.

WHY IS CALLIGRAPHY IMPORTANT?

The Prophet (PBUH) said, "Good writing is important because it makes the truth stand out." For Muslims, calligraphy (ornamental writing) is important because it carries the message of God. Calligraphers write in Arabic because this was the language in which the Koran wa... revealed. There are 29 letters in Arabic and it is written from right to left.

A Calligrapher ▲

This calligrapher in China is writing a notice in Arabic. In the past, calligraphers designed tiles showing words from the Koran, which were used to decorate mosques and important buildings.

Calligraphy Tools ▼

In the past, calligraphers used pens made from reeds and ink made from soot. They used a tiny mortar and pestle to crush the ingredients they needed to make colors

pen rest

pens

◀ Calligraphy Pictures

The picture on the left shows a man praying. The picture is actually made up of the words of the Shahada prayer (see page 8). Clever pictures like this, showing prayers or phrases such as "Allah is great" were very popular.

GABRIEL'S FIRST COMMAND

When the angel Gabriel visited Muhammad (PBUH), his first command was, "Read, in the name of Allah!" The words he read came from God and were later written down in the Koran. The words in the Koran always have to be spelled in exactly the same way, but calligraphers use many different types of decorative writing.

Everyday Objects ▶

Calligraphy brings God's word into everyday life when it is used on dishes and plates such as the one on the right. The writing is usually taken from the Koran and contains a blessing. Certain names of Allah, such as "The Healer" or "The Giver of Bread," are popular, too.

DO MUSLIMS LIKE STORIES?

Stories are an exciting way to tell people about Islamic leaders and their lives. During the month of Rabi-ul-Awwal, when the Prophet's (PBUH) birthday is celebrated, Muslims gather to tell stories about his life. Muslims also tell religious stories, which teach people how to live a good life.

◀ A Storyteller

A crowd of people gather to listen to a storyteller on a street in Marrakesh, Morocco. This is a common sight in Muslim countries, where storytelling is a popular entertainment. Tales of mystery and miracles, kings and their wars, and the lives of Islamic heroes all attract an audience.

THE ARABIAN NIGHTS

The *Arabian Nights* is a famous collection of folkloric tales. It includes the tales of Aladdin, Sinbad the sailor, and Ali Baba and the Forty Thieves. The collection was begun during the reign of the Khalifa Harun-ur-Rashid, who ruled in Baghdad between 786 and 809 C.E.

Moses (PBUH) and the Wise Man

This story is from a verse called "The Cave" in the Koran. It shows how things that appear strange can make sense, if only we can understand them properly.

Once, the Prophet Moses (PBUH) met a wise man, who had been given the gift of knowledge by Allah.

"Can I come with you and learn what you know?" Moses (PBUH) asked. The man replied, "You will not have the patience to watch me go about my business."

"I promise to be patient and obedient," said Moses (PBUH), and so the wise man agreed to let Moses (PBUH) go with him.

The wise man warned Moses (PBUH) not to ask him any questions. "I will tell you about things in my own time," he said.

Soon they came to a ship. The wise man made a hole in the bottom of it. "That is a strange thing to do!" Moses (PBUH) exclaimed. "Do you want to drown all the passengers?"

"I said you would lose patience with me," the old man said. Moses (PBUH) apologized and they continued on their journey. But Moses (PBUH) was astonished when they met a young man, and the wise man killed him. Once again, the wise man had to remind Moses (PBUH) not to lose patience with him.

They reached a town, but no one there would give them food and shelter. As they left, they saw a wall that was falling down.

The wise man stopped to mend it. "You could have asked for something in return," said Moses (PBUH).

The wise man replied, "We must now say goodbye to each other, but first I will explain my actions. I made the hole in the ship because a king wanted to take it away from the men who own it. It is no use to the king now, but the owners will be able to repair it.

"I killed the young man because he was going to bring dreadful suffering to his parents. Now they will have another son who will be good to them.

"As for the wall, there is treasure buried beneath it. It is Allah's will that two orphans will find the treasure when they grow up, because their father was a good man."

This story teaches us that wisdom and knowledge are rewards from Allah. They can be gained through patience, hard work, and faith.

◀ Shadow Puppets

Shadow puppets are often used to tell stories in Java. In the photograph on the left, they are being used to tell the story of Amir Hamza, the uncle of the Prophet (PBUH). He defended the Prophet (PBUH) with his life until he died in the battle of Badr. Muslim traders probably brought the story to Java at least two hundred years ago.

GLOSSARY

angel A messenger of God, created from light.

calligraphy Ornamental writing.

fast To go without food or drink.

Hadith Sayings of the Prophet (PBUH).

Hajj The pilgrimage to Mecca, which all Muslims should try to make at least once in their lives if they can afford it.

Hegira The Prophet Muhammad's (PBUH) journey from Mecca to Medina in 622 C.E.

Holy Haram The enclosed area around the Kaaba in Mecca.

Imam A Muslim religious leader.

incense A substance that gives off a sweet, spicy smell when it is burned.

Kaaba The black shrine in Mecca. Wherever they are in the world, Muslims turn to face the Kaaba during their daily prayers. They believe that it is the first place of worship God built on Earth.

Khalifa The title given to the leader of the Muslims, who was respected as the Prophet's (PBUH) representative. The Ommayad Khalifas were the descendants of Ali, the Prophet's (PBUH) son-in-law.

Koran (Qur'an) The Muslim holy book.

mihrab An arched alcove set into the wall of a mosque, which shows worshipers the direction of the Kaaba.

mosque The name for a Muslim place of worship.

pilgrimage A journey made for a religious reason, such as to visit a holy place.

Prophet (PBUH) Someone who speaks the words of God and is able to tell people what God wishes them to do. Muhammad (PBUH), the founder of Islam, is referred to as the Prophet (PBUH), but there are other Prophets (PBUH) in Islam, including Abraham (Ibrahim) (PBUH) and Moses (PBUH).

Ramadan The month during which Muslims fast between sunrise and sunset.

Salat The prayer ritual that is performed five times a day.

Shahada The declaration of Islamic faith, which expresses a Muslim's essential beliefs.

shrine A place where someone of extraordinary goodness is believed to have been buried.

Sufi A wise person who has devoted their life to worship and leads a simple life.

FURTHER READIN

American Islam: Growing Up Muslim in Ame
by Richard Wormser
(San Val, 2002)

Atlas of World Faiths: Islam
by Cath Senker
(Smart Apple Media, 2007)

Islam
by Jan Thompson
(Walrus Books, 2005)

INDEX

WEB SITES

Due to the changing nature of Internet links, Rosen Publishing has developed an online list of Web sites related to the subject of this book. This site is updated regularly. Please use this link to access this list: http://www.rosenlinks.com/wrel/isla